Disruptive Innovation

Disruptive Innovation

Rowan Everhart

CONTENTS

1 Introduction to Disruptive Innovation 1

2 Understanding the Impact of
Disruptive Innovation 5

3 Key Concepts in Disruptive
Innovation 9

4 Identifying Disruptive Opportunities 13

5 Strategies for Implementing
Disruptive Innovation 17

6 Managing Risk and Uncertainty 21

7 Measuring Success in Disruptive
Innovation 25

8 Case Studies of Successful
Disruptive Innovations 29

9 Ethical Considerations in Disruptive
Innovation 33

10 The Future of Disruptive Innovation 37

Introduction to Disruptive Innovation

M any traditional sectors in our modern industrial world are ill-equipped to cope with the pace, and quantity, of change now being forced upon them. Their organization, business processes, and installed technology systems are all remnants of an industrial age now disappearing over the horizon. The pressures to innovate speedily are creating threats to incumbents, but also great opportunities for those who can master disruptive innovation. What is now critical is the recognition that the forces which generations of entrepreneurs and corporate giants of the later half of the past century learned to exploit are now different. The effective management of innovation has become the key to business success in the twenty-first century, and this article offers guidelines and insights to help executives adjust.

It has become a truism that business operations are speeding up and that ever shorter product life cycles are the norm. But the pace of change is not just getting faster; it is accelerating. Entire industries are facing radical, exponential change and are being transformed out of all recognition by what is called disruptive innovation. We all recognize the attributes of internet services, such as blogs, web-based email, or online movies, that compete with conventional media products (print and broadcast) or business models with such ferocity that they are obliterating, or at least transforming, them. The same phenomena are reshaping other sectors such as software, mini-computers, and telecoms, while completely new products or concepts are changing our behavior in areas as diverse as music, leisure, and the environment.

Defining Disruptive Innovation

This confusion is inevitable: we humans are hard-wired to over-generalize from experience. Consequently, when future events occur that are related in any way to a past experience, but are not the conventional extensions or uses of the innovation that is the subject of the past experience, we are sorely tempted to describe the event as "disruptive". In fact, the word allows us to keep one foot straddling the past and one foot straddling the future; people from the past don't have to cast aside the habits, thinking, and rules of conduct that have made them successful. Rather, they express cautious public support for the innovation in question, attending to their more immediate breadwinning with the resources and wit to straddle both worlds. They can be, if it were, simultaneously against and for a new approach.

In 1995, I coined the term "disruptive technology" to describe a new technology that unexpectedly displaces an established technology. This theory has become a powerful tool for business managers to battle the status quo. The term is now found in patents, court opinions, and management writings. Unfortunately, "disruptive technology" has escaped its moorings and is serving to describe even the most trivial of changes to products. There are those, for example, who claim that the introduction of tax software was a disruptive technology. I've been working hard to help intelligent people consistently distinguish between processes that should be labeled disruptive from those that are routine, evolving, sustaining advances, and even non-events.

Historical Examples of Disruptive Innovation

Early steam engines were used to pump water out of mines and to power mills. They were often of limited power and speed, and much effort was spent by deriving better, cheaper ways to produce them. The story of how George Stephenson won the important contract for building this classic first passenger railroad contains several points of interest. One is that the entire idea of building the world's first railroad was considered laughably absurd. The other is that the Parliament required for such an eccentric and suicidal idea to obtain approval from Parliament decreed that there must be a man with a red flag walking in front of it, warning people that such a monstrous beast was bearing down on them. This was not an economically healthy mandate. Yet it was initially essential to allow the railroad to be created. It could not have been created without getting this mandate. Simply being disruptive, simply creeping up the right hand side of this graph, isn't enough. In the end, the railroad wasn't disruptive, it was transformative.

Historical examples of disruptive innovation. Historically, disruptive innovations have typically been simpler and less sophisticated than the traditional technology. Disruptive innovations often enable less skilled labor to perform tasks that historically could only be completed by highly skilled, more expensive labor. In the automobile industry, for example, the Ford Model T was very simple compared to others currently available at the time, and made the technology available to a less wealthy class of buyers. Thousands of other businesses made their money modifying the "Tin Lizzie" with different configurations, as the supply for customer demand (including police cars and pick-up trucks).

Understanding the Impact of Disruptive Innovation

What drives the evolution of technology? Disruptive innovations emerge from arena, value networks linking technologies and markets. Erroneously, companies are likely to perceive emergent paths to disruptive innovation leading both upmarket and downstream from the company's own products. Official strategies that advocate building on current competencies might lead to making it harder to follow the emergent paths to disruptive innovation. Rather than getting bogged down in visioning exercises, technology entrepreneurs should remain alert to the unexpected inroads of disruptive innovation. Be where the action is, where emergent paths to disruptive innovation become visible, and create an environment that is conducive to thinking about technology and markets in unconventional ways.

Disruptive innovation, a particular causal mechanism of change that has been responsible for the rise and fall of businesses throughout history, has three distinct characteristics that are the dimensions of this model. Disruptive innovations are simpler and more convenient products or services that may not appear as attractive as existing offerings to people who have more money than time. Disruptive innovations start by addressing markets where the alternatives are none or indifferent. Once the disruptive innovation gains a foothold in these markets, they can improve their performance and move up-market to address more demanding customers. However, the very capabilities that are praised by leading customers have driven the disruptive innovator and its customers out of the business. Disruptive innovation shapes the evolution of markets.

Economic Implications

On balance, technological determinism might be characterized as placing primary emphasis on the ability of technology to displace people. Recognizing the needs and potential benefits of displaced workers is seen as fundamental to the notion of technological determinism, which emphasizes government investment in human resources and transitional support. Any erosion of the rights of workers resulting from this changing social contract is attributed solely to the "power over" determination of a technology-controlled few. Other exponents of technological determinism are amplifying the potential disruptive consequences of future technologies that involve human interaction while focusing on performing numerous critical tasks and jobs.

When powerful economic interests understand an important issue, they usually find a way of turning the thinking about the problem to their advantage. In contemporary discussion of competitiveness and economic growth, two views of technology and economic development have emerged. The philosophy and theory of technological determinism see technology in ways that pose the greatest potential threat to conservative interests. Influence is the key element in turning technological change to the task of increasing productivity. Technology is viewed as an external force acting upon a passive society. Here, governments, business leaders, and average citizens are primarily interested in managing those technologies to gain the greatest good for the greatest number.

Social and Cultural Effects

Social and cultural traditions lie at the core of the issue of distributing innovation. While it is difficult to discard a long-held belief, 'faith-based technology' shows that it is possible when the belief in the traditional solution to a problem today is severely affected by modern society. Rodgers & Thorson have proposed a six-point theory of innovation that holds that a message must follow a path of overcoming (1) Awareness, (2) Agree, (3) Self-efficacy, (4) Outcomes, (5) Individual adoption and (6) Social systems adoption. The rate of adoption will be affected by complexity, relative advantage, compatibility, trialability, and observability. In particular, trialability and observability are effectively time scales of adoption, compatibility affects the magnitude of contribution providing support during redefinition and self-efficacy, trust and referred to as 'cosmothetic' innovation in discussions of semi 'technically driven' innovation.

Another criticism of adoption is based upon the social and traditional ties that a customer has to existing products and services. The customer product life cycle model described in Chapter 6 shows how, to the customer, (A) a need is derived from a specific tradition, (B) it is initially satisfied by a product, (C) the satisfaction provided by that product over its life varies, finally (D) the need is once again derived from a revised tradition that includes the incorporated source of satisfaction provided by the discontinued product. Innovations that attach themselves too closely to a previous tradition or satisfy a need too well when the existing solution is considered adequate impede or block adoption. While changes in need can be planned for, culturally inspired traditions are difficult to change and, consequently, would appear to be major barriers to the introduction of new products.

Key Concepts in Disruptive Innovation

The seasoned board chairs and CEOs of established corporations to whom I speak typically turn to me and ask, "Is that what a disruptive innovation is? Do I need to worry about them now?" At a first glance, the concept of disruptive innovation seems straightforward. Yet despite the simplicity and unmistakable power of the theory, there is much confusion and disagreement about the helpfulness and accuracy of the term. Indeed, the incorrect identification of disruptive innovations often results in decisions that do more harm than good: managers allocate capital to projects that are unlikely ever to offer profitable returns, and public policy makers encourage the certainty of financial distress by subsidizing companies with great need but little chance of leading a rebuilding of the economy.

What is disruptive innovation? According to the professor and author Clayton Christensen, disruptive innovation "describes a process by which a product or service takes root initially in simple applications at the bottom of a market and then relentlessly moves up market, eventually displacing established competitors." In Christensen's original research, this process was often the story of new entrants attacking incumbents by developing products and services that were simpler, cheaper, and often more convenient to use.

Sustaining Innovation vs Disruptive Innovation

Innovative growth, as part of a strategy based on the development of products, services, and markets, is often severely restricted. The result is that the potential for the full exploitation of the relevance and reach of the core technologies in new areas is diminished. Consequently, whilst remaining defenseless against the attack of other companies' disruptive technologies, these core technologies become increasingly difficult to sustain and defend. In the technology-based sector, all the drivers behind sustaining success - technology quality, development process efficiency, cost of delivery and scale, and raw, financial, and time invested - often create bricks in the walls of the mainstream castle, raising the drawbridge.

The drivers behind sustained success and subsequent archetypal building and reinforcement behaviors often hinder the discovery and development of businesses at the margins. The very rational, financial, and process-oriented developments of maturity are often exactly the antithesis of those characteristics required for the development of the associated products, services, and markets.

The Innovator's Dilemma

The term disruptive innovation was coined and its application explained, a commonly used one by the Harvard economist Clayton M. Christensen and his colleagues. They brought to the public's attention profit- and agenda-wrecking dynamics once known only to the small fragment of the business world that experienced it or that had the vision and courage to embrace the risks inherent to being a serious, well-informed first mover. If the commercial landscape with which senior executives worked had changed slowly and predictably, we would not have called for them to transform the management of their organizations. But the swift and relentless trajectory of technological change has shortened the lives of even the world's most successful public companies to a few decades, rather than a century or more. If the roles of senior executives are to be more than brief stepping stones to retirement or, more frequently, a necessary introduction to a new member with confidence and vision, the management of organizational innovation must evolve.

Innovators can use disruptive technologies to create new growth by breathing life into new or underperforming markets. Here, our concern is the threat of disruptive technology. This usually happens when new entrants with new technology target low-end customers or unserved ones, resulting in rust from high-end incumbents. The dilemma is that companies that have invested, sometimes for decades, in listening to their most profitable customers and ignoring the rest are tine, when they should be most able to respond. They are almost always successfully disrupted. In response to a material threat to its value-growth potential, senior management must align the organization's motivations and rewards systems and invest to listen systematically to those who shape its future. They must also look at industry evolution and the role of entrant versus incumbent. These are lessons from the success stories of those who have met and exceeded the expectations of both value and growth.

4 |

Identifying Disruptive Opportunities

Successful innovation requires finding the right discovery logic for turning new technologies into new products and services and identifying whether or not businesses already have disruptive strategies underway. It is about gaining foresight. To do so, companies must not only know how to innovate but also why, where, what, how, and with whom. Knowing why, where, what, how, and with whom — together with the new knowledge that stream lengths beyond maturity do indeed foster global industry structures — enables innovators to use the theory of disruption to discover when opportunities might occur and understanding discover opportunities and strategies on other disruptions already in place.

Innovators are well served working smarter as opposed to harder. Smart innovators address disruptions by targeting products and services at the point on the value ladder in which customers are overserved at the right price point. New markets can also be discovered by taking simplifying value propositions from technologies in the middle of their disruptive cycles. At more advanced stages of disruptive cycles, innovators can uncover additional disruptable innovation opportunities by identifying principles: return on gross assets and gross margin consistency, tailoring business models to a particular class of competition, and concentrating on a niche in a market that is unserved.

Market Research Techniques

One of the most common mistakes in market forecasting is the use of "demand forecasting tools" without any attention to the concepts and underlying principles behind the tools themselves. For example, it isn't possible to properly model the future size of a market without having a valid understanding of the determinants of fertility rates and life expectancies. Without this understanding and appreciation for the driving forces behind population growth and distribution, economists are likely to make poor assumptions and under- or overstate their forecasts. Likewise, it doesn't make sense to attempt to model the size of a market by failing to recognize any potential spillover effects of one segment of the market onto another because alternative resources aren't priced in the market. In this example, failing to understand the roles of transformation aids and substitutes isn't likely to lead to accurate forecasts of future market responses and evolution.

One of the most effective tools for successful strategic and marketing planning and operation is economic forecasting. However, the acquisition of adequate inputs, the proper treatment of those inputs, and the attainment of meaningful conclusions from a good economic model are not trivial tasks. By no means can they be accomplished simply by anyone with access to a computer and the software required to run the modeling programs. Nonetheless, most current theoretically and empirically validated models, especially those based on the structural equation formula or other dynamic formulations, need not be puzzling to relatively non-technical audiences.

Any serious market research should be based on a solid understanding of the underlying economics of a business or industry. All too often, however, estimates of market size and growth and forecasts of consumer demand and behavior are not grounded in any conceptual framework of how markets work. This is ironic because industry economics and business strategy are, in many ways, the natural ends of the information-search process. Their onus rests squarely on studying the basic forces that shape demand and thereby influence prices and market dynamics.

Customer Needs Analysis

Accordingly, a company must orient its processes around solving a problem, rather than simply selling a product. Firms need to ask the question: what are their funders hiring it to do? While this can be a difficult question to answer, doing so can greatly increase the likelihood that a firm will be successful and not fall before a disruptive innovation. On the whole, by offering more than they really need or can profitably sell, organizations dilute their simplicity and often lose the confidence of potential customers. Concentration on the quality-price trade-off will lead to poor decisions about new-product development. Should Motorola be introduced a pager that was half as reliable as it was discourtesy radar detector? Ignore the products, figure out the job to be done, and then meet the critical performance point for a segment of the market that has previously been overserved by existing players in the market and under or overlooked by those same participants.

Instead of vacillating about consumers' trade-offs between quality and price, or discussing the extent to which consumers are rationally rather than emotionally motivated, marketing and strategic planners would find the disruptive technology theory easier to apply by thinking more clearly about what they sell. Simply put, they sell jobs to be done. The underlying reason customers make the trade-offs between quality and price is that they need to get certain jobs done and they will hire those products or services that help them get those jobs done most easily and inexpensively.

5

Strategies for Implementing Disruptive Innovation

Regardless of the specific goals that a company is working to accomplish, they all must conceptualize the environment in which they are operating, define what success actually means, and determine what kind of structures are needed. This brings us back to the classic strategy formulation approach that we described earlier. Companies must choose where they want to compete, how they expect to win, and what are the desired results. In that framework, we uncovered two overarching principles that will lead to intelligent responses. These are two of our earlier proposed seven maxims which suggest not to let what you know limit what you can imagine, and that there are no bad technologies, only bad people.

As we analyze case studies of companies that successfully implemented disruptive innovation, we use the framework set out earlier to define the variables that led to their success. Our intent is to better understand the streams of thought that informed their strategies. Their responses often defy classical management principles and are most usefully reported as practices rather than as principles to be followed that could lead others to miss their goals. On the other hand, we find that very popular management maxims were not necessarily relevant for successful attacking. The result is a different approach to thinking about success under conditions of technological change.

Agile Development Processes

We first consider some of the performance pressures that push businesses into having their development efforts flock to a new external innovation process. The problems faced by many businesses in trying to implement this eco-friendly approach are well documented. Then, recognizing this is an increasingly important focus for many businesses, our discussion moves to identifying necessary IT capabilities - knowing what works, why certain things work, and what the outcomes of trying different strategies might be in a range of business areas. High corporate social responsibility is taken as given. After this, a proven approach to ensuring that an agile business can stay ahead of its competition is outlined. Small businesses who implement solutions like the ones presented can throw long shadows. The use of technology in the innovation process can be profitable for all parties involved. The chapter concludes with a series of case studies that illustrate how many businesses are focusing their development efforts on customer-informed innovation processes and how many stagger as they attempt the delicate dance of relationship building with external business partners.

Adaptable businesses move beyond traditional development processes to adopt a new environmentally aware innovation process that minimizes manufacturing costs. These businesses also establish partnerships with not just suppliers but customers as well to streamline how they exchange products and services. What this environmental awareness leads to over time is a more powerful organization and a more collaborative business network, a highly effective combination that creates significant strategic advantage. By focusing on using only the resources they need, the requirements of the business units themselves in terms of such things as cost pressures, global competition, and IT security, businesses can take the most cost-effective route to producing what the customers want. The use of innovative technologies to map the business ecosystem, coupled with the careful and deliberate focus on strategic innovation, leads to agile development processes that produce only the most relevant and highest quality customer services.

Cross-Functional Teams

But cross-functional teams are also the nerve center for an efficient flow of information about the marketplace and about the firm's capabilities. Most important, they are the source of the interactions with the "ba" or "rich context" of the Kyokankakatsu approach discussed in the second chapter. And many companies find that cross-functional teams can redouble the voices and contributions of the few customers or prospective customers who are present in the marketplace. The persistence of traditional functional departments, however, means that management has to know how to set up conditions so that this knowledge in the group truly becomes a form of business research.

Cross-functional teams are essential for effectively managing the tensions and tasks associated with innovation projects. The people on such teams have dual reporting structures: they report to both the innovation project manager and their home department managers. In our experience, cross-functional teams are usually the steel spine of innovation that allows the project manager to maintain the pace of development without becoming the bottleneck.

6

Managing Risk and Uncertainty

The second method for managing risk is preferable. Increasing capacity can become an end in itself, leading to a system where firms without a good use for their premier technologies "burn capital" that would be better used elsewhere. Decreasing investment size allows us to assemble highly effective firms, funded on a just-in-time basis, redefining the firm as a systems integrator and choreographer. The firm of the future will not perform the magic (otherwise known as hiring a few research and development people) in long research programs, visible in five-year product plans. The firm of the future will redefine itself as a master in the art of the transfer of technology, working with an increasing number of firms all around the world. We need to know how to knit a few stitches and computer information systems tightly in order to ensure that the resulting global pattern is truly superior.

In an age of unpredictable business cycles, disruptive change, and dangerous accelerating complexity, there are only two ways to manage an increasing amount of risk. The first way is to increase your risk-bearing capacity. Easier said than done. For firms with large amounts of product life cycle risk and decreasing investment horizons, increasing risk-bearing capacity is a huge drain on resources, usually through resorting to a policy of mergers and acquisitions.

The second way to manage risk is to decrease investment size. Funds needed for investment during times of accelerating change, uncertainty, and risk must be used ever more wisely. This is one important reason why small venture capital-funded development projects can effectively compete with internal corporate research and development.

Scenario Planning

Although scenario planning forces management to think about the future, it can be an expensive and time-consuming process. Collecting the data on alternatives, analyzing the implications of these alternatives, and developing strategic responses can be overwhelming. Once again, managers are better advised to live in the future as in parallel businesses, customer research, current strategic initiatives, the planner's employment, and the planning process. These may reveal as much useful information to better alternatives. With the extensive amount of data from the developments, it is easier to find patterns that might indicate the future. In addition, many firms do not use alternative scenarios and stick to the traditional strategic models. Even when assigned scenarios are developed, Shanley indicates that in the best organizations, the scenarios are considered only one input to the planning process.

Scenario planning involves coming up with probable alternative, future environments for the firm. Most scenario planning is performed using two critical scenario dimensions: levels of industry driving forces and concentration of mass. Examples of industry driving forces include: technological change, globalization, market forces, pace of change, and public policy. Levels of concentration represent the participants within a given industry, including: industry convergence, new competitors, and changing roles of the current participants, number of dominant players, and industry polarization between a few very large firms and a fragmented group of small firms. The objective of the scenario planning is to generate a number of different, crucial worldviews about the identified changes. Once this view or views of the future are created and agreed upon, strategies to address these issues are developed.

Risk Mitigation Strategies

Innovation tends to be a riskier business than cash harvest. Navigating the minefield of disruptive innovation requires not only good theory and framework but also thoughtful judgment in dealing with unknowns, uncertainties, and naysayers. Counterintuitively, two common but flawed strategies actually exacerbate uncertainties and generally result in the innovation being more disruptive to the investor than to the market. Such suboptimal strategies increase corporate risk exposure right at the time an investor should be doing the reverse: reducing risk exposure to a level deemed acceptable given the capabilities and resources of the firm. On the other hand, the use of a particular risk mitigation strategy should not be viewed as an endorsement of an under-investment in innovation either, as that would pose its own kind of risk.

Innovation invariably involves unknowns at the outset. After all, that is why it is called innovation. Unfortunately, the degree of unknowns is often amplified when the innovation tackles non-consumption or the creation of a new market. In these situations, one fundamental problem is that managers often demand the same types of returns and controls from innovations that a cash-harvesting-oriented investment would provide. This explains why innovation – and investment in innovation – is often insufficient within established firms.

7

Measuring Success in Disruptive Innovation

We have created little or no systematic techniques to measure a manager's success in achieving disruptive growth inside their organizations. Concepts like "maximizing shareholder value," "total cost of ownership," "balancing stakeholders' interest," and "outsourcing" are not quantifiable measures that a manager can use to manage the day-to-day activities of their people. On any one particular day, on what basis, exactly, would we claim success? If understanding and managing disruptive innovation as a quantifiable outcome is something we really seek to do, we must move beyond rhetoric and metaphor and define atomic components of the ecosystem that have a score in Abraham Maslow's lower and surely important needs of organizational managers: food, air, water, and sex.

In the preceding chapters, we described the dilemma that established companies find themselves in when confronting disruptive change. Focusing excessively on customers' needs and existing products can conveniently explain why few companies prosper from disruptive innovation. Some managers observe that shareholders are served well by established companies going up-market to position themselves as "solutions" providers, but very few legendary companies are written into history by the market. However, just as it's possible to get too comfortable with a product or with a particular set of customers, one can get comfortable becoming a truly great company in a particular industry, going up-market. The financial and emotional rewards associated with becoming a truly great company in one's specific arena are compelling enough to lure a great many companies down the path of market over-expansion.

Key Performance Indicators

Once the strategic initiatives and KPIs are in place, the tool with which to begin the implementing process is the Kaizen program. With an assigned goal, a team identifies underlying agreements causing inhibition of a performance level consistent with the strategic initiative. Then with a rapid application of principle-based, data-driven improvement efforts, results are produced in a short time frame. Analysis and improvements are implemented, followed by testing to confirm the improvement represents a step change, and then shifting to testing and deployment on a broader scale.

The critical suggested KPIs for enabling disruptive innovation are: - New growth, meaningful experimentation, and novel business models that acknowledge that the future is uncertain, and that the organization can learn from mistakes, both successful and unsuccessful. - Customer, partner, and key employee satisfaction levels that are promising indicators of progress along the enabling disruptive innovation journey. - Relative profit improvement compared to industry peers.

Key performance indicators (KPIs) are critical measures of the strategic initiatives, providing focus and momentum for the people in the organization. The KPIs must represent causes of business success - drivers of financial performance, not the results themselves. It is a mistake to substitute benefit-cost or internal efficiency measures for strategic KPIs. KPIs can be both short-term or long-term, but what they must have in common is that they measure the effectiveness of the key business processes as they relate to strategic initiatives. To be useful, KPIs need to include targets and involve business managers using these KPIs to drive improvement.

Success Metrics

The potential of intelligent agents in the information world is immense. Every time I pay my property taxes, which remain low because all sorts of neighbors share the cost, I think about an article that he told me about its job as a property tax assessor. I fantasize an intelligent agent that would consider the article and other information available to it, introduce a levy, and in thousands of millisecond-long telephone calls to assessors remind them of their responsibilities to check property values and measure well-deserved taxes on all those wealthy homeowners behind the condos next door.

The balancing act on the path of disruptive innovation, then, is to achieve the learning that returns from commercial feedback at the least possible cost. Yet how is it possible to outrun competition without the strength of the existing business to back up aggressive growth? The first secret lies in different success metrics. Sure, financial success is important, and hanging by that thread is backbreaking work. Yet the primary success metric for a growth KBA is learning, not earnings, faith in the future and not faith in the present. Success, in turn, is not building architecture and systems that will withstand the barrage of today's customer requirements, but imagining future systems with all sorts of flexible features and then learning which ones to build and when to build them.

8 |

Case Studies of Successful
Disruptive Innovations

A detailed study of these three successful disruptive innovations shows that, on the industry level, commercial success from providing electronic information services in these new areas to businesses will change as industries' artifact concentrations change. The internet has significant changes in where artifacts get created and who uses them because portals make everyone easily aware of everyone else's public artifacts. Disruptive innovations build new industries and affect the motivation and rewards of all players, not just those who provide and use the disruptive innovations and associated business models.

This chapter examines three case studies of successful disruptive innovations: department stores, discount retailing, and mini-mills. In contrast to the radio, these innovations were, for the most part, non-electronic in nature. Yet, they suggest several powerful principles for digital-based changes as well. All three were extremely successful. In each case, they both attacked, crippled, and rejuvenated the incumbent industry. The innovations helped to change the meaning of 'shopping', 'retail', and 'steel'. They changed when, how, and why customers shop at all these places. They also changed the organization, roles, and responsibilities of the buildings and employees at all these places. Additionally, they created an industry super-power. In short, all three resulted in durable, value-creating market economies through building new networks and artifacts. Disruptive innovations, then, are important in their own right, regardless of their motivations, because successful disruptive innovators become leaders.

Uber

The result is that initially Uber's driver corps of independent operators, which has since grown internationally, collectively outperforms traditional providers, which struggle in comparison, by the relevant metrics of frequency, responsiveness, quality, and overall experience. Just like the EC2 instances of its technology forebear, Uber's intelligent cloud-based allocation of human resources during seasonal peaks, events, and times of day struggles and sometimes occasionally fails to take into account worker supply and customer demand patterns that aren't apparent until they are figured out the hard way—usually when it starts getting busy—precisely like its techie forebears. And just like Airbnb's prosumer accommodations aren't always quite up to the experience of chain hotel professionals, there are indeed quiet, comfortable limousine services dispatching only modern Lincoln and Cadillac vehicles, and well-trained drivers who will take you around the city and elsewhere and be there even if it starts raining heavily on these services' slickly mobile-friendly websites.

Uber is designed around a couple of simple but profound innovations. The first is that it utilizes a previously untapped source of high-quality labor, people who already own their own cars. By tapping these people—anyone with a clean driving record, an automobile, and a smartphone—Uber can avoid the regulatory, safety, and fixed-cost burdens that traditional taxi or limousine services face.

This, in turn, allows Uber to provide faster, more convenient, and more reliable service, which in cities where it is available has been transformative. Furthermore, Uber contracts with people for whom driving is often already second nature and who thus exhibit a casual street literacy: abilities and cultural instincts that have not only been honed over years or a lifetime but are difficult to teach or qualify more uniformly.

Uber illustrates several key advantages and strategies that can make incumbent organizations more resilient, if not yet antifragile, or enable entrants to disrupt and build rapidly using the modern infrastructure and opportunities for social distillation that the cloud enables.

Airbnb

The key to its success encapsulates the essence of the formula to survive and thrive in a rapidly changing world. Airbnb has introduced an online hospitality service acting as a broker for property owners and vacationers who are cost and an interesting experience-conscious and who value social interactivity, local knowledge, personal awareness and control, and festive events to the virtual hotel offered by the traditional care-on-the-side-of-cost major booking agencies. We are interested in how to thrive and survive in the real world. The (strong) presence of this valuable co-dynamic is noteworthy. Providing a warm welcome, always there for us, and focused on quality of service for all can be treated as a necessary attribute within a priority grid of real world sensitivities. What this means for the survival of key traditional hotels is important to identify, singularly, and in a broader context within the strategic industries of a nation.

Disruptive innovations in the form of new business models have destroyed relatively young and prosperous industries like the record companies and created brilliant wealth, such as in the cases of Google and Facebook. Airbnb, established in 2008, and with an estimated value in 2018 of over 30 billion USD and approval ratings for successful hosting in Spain of ca. 7.3/10 and 80% favorable comments, is a stunning example of clever business model innovation. It did not invent the sharing economy, but it has represented the concept in the finest possible way.

9

Ethical Considerations in Disruptive Innovation

It is important, then, that managers consciously monitor the ethical implications of their innovative strategies and are prepared to alter or abstain from activities that transgress the well-being of others. It is also important for both management and their stakeholders to openly discuss innovative strategies in order to curtail concerns that might otherwise escalate to potentially costly and harmful disputes. Social and legal frameworks that guide the actions of managers can also help to protect the rights of society's stakeholders and prevent the erosion of a firm's license to innovate.

In recognizing both the opportunities and the requirements for disruptive innovation, managers must also be vigilant about the ethical, legal, and social implications of their strategies. Understanding that the pursuit of disruptive innovation can yield tremendous benefits for both industry and society, the prospect of eroded capabilities and established relationships is often the concern both internally and externally.

The preceding pages provide an in-depth examination of the phenomenon of disruptive innovation and strategies for applying a framework to profit from it. We have illustrated business models and strategies that are particularly appropriate for use in exploiting the asymmetries faced by incumbent market leaders.

Privacy Concerns

New York University professor Danah Boyd has pointed out that marginalized communities often cannot use the same cybersecurity measures as others because their interventions attract others' attention or need proxies that can make use of sophisticated privacy protection tools. Tailoring the point of privacy protection, being able to turn it off and on, and granting some others access to its benefits in certain situations is necessary in order to balance factors such as safety and security against privacy. After all, intimacy with a machine boosting privacy in one specific context can also be considered a kind of privacy violation. Devices collecting personal data can all too easily become so close to us that we prefer to treat the problem as hard.

The starting point of a good ethics checklist is user control. People should have the right to refuse participation in data collection and to edit or delete personal data that is currently in use. The people behind the data must also be informed about how their information is being collected and used and against whom it is being compared and tested. Anonymity - or the use of non-personal data - should always be the first option whenever use of the data is feasible. Today, data breaches are monitored by interconnected customers relying on digital services. In addition, the integrity of privacy-protecting algorithms must be continuously evaluated by independent experts.

Fair Competition

1) The tests for fairness and pro-competitive behavior should be well-understood and easy to explain. 2) Laws that have been written

to block certain behavior should be reviewed with an eye towards setting up tests for fairness and pro-competitive behavior, and made more objective. Laws like the US antitrust laws are in need of such an update. 3) Efforts should be made to anticipate the shape of proper test. The goal should be laws that make it easy to answer the questions: When has an organization won with more skill? When has it worked more cleverly? What is fair? What is right? What is pro-competitive? What is in the public interest?

Supportive regulations and laws are of great importance if individuals, companies, universities, and government agencies are going to be seen as contributing to the societal imperative of economic development. Whether one is concerned about large, established enterprises, disruptive innovators, new start-ups, universities, trade associations, not-for-profit research organizations, or government funding agencies, the laws and regulations need review and update. Here are a few principles and laws that should be kept in mind.

10

The Future of Disruptive
Innovation

Disruptive innovation is a useful concept for interpreting the problems to which companies have been forced to respond. It provides a warning that bad things are happening, and helps to associate together apparently disconnected events into a coherent perspective. It suggests that all the warning signs - the management style that encourages the servicing of large clients and the maintenance of historic franchises as opposed to exploring the full potential of new innovations, the universalization of a single way of doing things, the burdensome financial structure - are the symptoms of a deeper problem, which can become fatal.

That's our view of the world. What is striking is the absence of a compelling response to the problem of obsolescence. Companies don't set out to become large, constipated organizations that are unable to embrace new technologies and new markets, defend their franchises or meet the needs of society. Long-established companies don't wake up in the morning and decide that the only winning move is not to play. But rather than take defensive action, they seem all too often to be overwhelmed and belated. We think defensive action is indeed possible. Management science and strategy are, in our view, in a position to provide clear guidelines on when and how to change course. And organizations can, we believe, be geared to manage the risk of obsolescence.

Emerging Technologies

Ultra Capacitors - Ultra Capacitors save electricity and are less than the size of a television remote control. They are better than batteries and they will soon have the ability to run an electric car 50 miles on the energy saved from a 10-foot long rubber track. -Textures - Today, textures "produced" include arrays of nano- and micro-scale pillars, walls, ridges or ridges. These textures in turn "produce" ultrahydrophobic (self-cleaning) surfaces and their UV resistant and scratch-resistant antireflection coated windows. This technology is ready for commercialization in all of these areas. The development of SST variations is also quite straightforward for solar cells, large area windows, and scratch-resistant coatings.

In this chapter, we'll explore some of the main emerging technologies, all of which have the potential to dramatically alter the competitive landscape over the coming decade. But unlike the pointless debates that arise over whether technological innovation is wholly disruptive or not, the implications of the spread and adoption of these technologies make for fascinating material. The most significant coming disruption to the basic structures of business and society are three technologies: Micro-electro-mechanical systems (MEMS) are popping up everywhere, often when their effect is least expected. MEMS are variously small mechanics on a silicon chip, or more prosaically, small devices. Nanotechnology refers to the ability to put single molecules in specific places, and to make materials from those molecules.

Global Trends

Global innovation is not about abandoning "old" lines of production imports to "new," low-cost suppliers in the East. It is about managing a complex multidomestic strategy in which companies must be as concerned with local R&D requirements as they are concerned with local, low-cost manufacturing, assembly, and sales and distribution. It is about working with the best in the world to craft, maintain, and compete in the world's best supply chains. These supply chains are often clusters of companies with complementary capabilities that work together to mass customize established product lines and computer-integration capabilities. The same is true for product development and related services. These clusters, in turn, require the presence of significant critical masses in specialized research topics in which clusters meet or exceed the global state of the art. Leaders use such critical masses and other necessary supporting institutions to manage a portfolio of activities to leverage global technology in line with their strategic objectives.

"The Rise of the East," in which author Amitav Acharya sums up an important global trend: the rise of Asia and, more generally, the resurgence of the world's emerging economies. Archarya notes that in historical terms, the ascent of Asia has been surprisingly sudden. As recently as 1980, notes Archarya, "no Asian state figured in the list of the world's ten largest economies as measured in terms of gross domestic product [but] in 2005, Japan, China, and India had muscled their way into it." In fact, between 1960 and 2000, both Japan and the region's newly industrializing countries grew at such a torrid pace that, as Archarya writes, "Japan managed the rare feat of overtaking advanced industrial countries, including the United States, while the four 'Asian Tigers' - Hong Kong, Singapore, South Korea, and Taiwan - improved business and finance daily."